HOOD COUNTY PUBLIC LIBRARY
101448

AF579966

GUINNESS BOOK OF PHENOMENAL HAPPENINGS

Shahid Malik performed an escape from a straight-jacket while he was suspended from a helicopter 1,160 feet above the ground over West Yorkshire, England, on July 12, 1975.

GUINNESS BOOK OF PHENOMENAL HAPPENINGS

BY NORRIS McWHIRTER & ROSS McWHIRTER

Illustrated by Kenneth Laager

STERLING PUBLISHING CO., INC. NEW YORK

OTHER BOOKS OF INTEREST

Guinness Book of Amazing Achievements
Guinness Book of Astounding Feats and Events
Guinness Book of Olympic Records
Guinness Book of Phenomenal Happenings
Guinness Book of World Records
Guinness Book of Young Recordbreakers
Guinness Sports Record Book

Fourth Printing, 1977

Two Park Avenue, New York, N.Y. 10016
Based on the Guinness Book of World Records

Manufactured in the United States of America

Library of Congress Catalog Card No.: 76–1162
Sterling ISBN 0-8069-0040–7 Trade
0041–5 Library

INTRODUCTION

Unusual or unique happenings can be more astounding than fiction or fantasy. After 20 years of combing the world for the most phenomenal happenings for the GUINNESS BOOK OF WORLD RECORDS, we realize that some of the happenings included in this book seem unbelievable.

We want to assure our readers, however, that every happening illustrated is true and accurate. You can believe every statement made, for we have checked and authenticated everything.

NORRIS McWHIRTER and ROSS McWHIRTER

What country eats the most candy? The biggest consumers of candy are the people of Britain with 7.8 oz. of candy per person per week. The people of Scotland alone have a higher per capita average—9 oz. of candy a week.

The most common disease in the world is tooth decay, which affects over 53 per cent of the population of the United States. Few people ever completely escape having some cavities during their lifetime.

Emitt Peters won the 1975 running of the annual 1,049-mile dog sled race from Anchorage to Nome, Alaska in a record time – 14 days 14 hours 43 minutes.

Dogs rarely live more than 20 years. A black Labrador gun dog named "Adjutant" lived under the care of his owner, James Hawkes, from his birth on August 14, 1936, to his death on November 20, 1963 – more than 27 years. It's a world record for dogs.

The largest pizza ever baked measured 25 feet across, was 494 square feet in area, and weighed 1,200 lbs. It was baked at the Pizza Inn, Little Rock, Arkansas, on September 4, 1974.

Hattiesburg, Mississippi, claims the largest hamburger ever recorded. For this hamburger, the cooks used 230 lbs. of beef, 4 gallons of tomato sauce, a gallon of mustard, and buns 14 feet across. A beefburger made in Blackpool, England, in March, 1975, was larger, however, weighing 440 lbs. and measuring 15 feet in diameter.

Rising 630 feet above the city of St. Louis, Missouri, the Gateway Arch is the world's tallest monument. Completed on October 28, 1965, the sweeping stainless steel arch was designed by Eero Saarinen. It commemorates the westward expansion of the United States after the Louisiana Purchase of 1803.

The largest advertising sign ever erected was the electric Citroën sign on the Eiffel Tower in Paris, which was first switched on on July 4, 1925. It was lit up with 250,000 individual lamps in six colors and could be seen 24 miles away. The letter "N" alone measured 68 feet 5 inches high.

The most remote lighthouse is called The Smalls and is located about 16 sea miles (18.4 land miles) off the coast of Wales.

The loneliest tree in the world, the one most distant from any other, is believed to be the one at an oasis in the Tenere Desert in the Niger Republic in Africa. There are no other trees within 31 miles, yet in February, 1960, a truck driver ran into it.

Reaching almost $2\frac{1}{2}$ miles (actually 12,600 feet) into the earth is the world's deepest mine, the Western Deep Levels Mine in South Africa. At such extreme depths cool air has to be brought in to offset the heat of the rocks, which reaches 126° F. Rock bursts due to the pressure are another great danger.

Some volcanoes stop being active for long periods of time, lying dormant but always capable of coming back to life. The highest such dormant volcano is Volcán Llullaillaco, which rises to a height of 22,058 feet on the border between Chile and Argentina in South America.

The first person to row across the Atlantic from West to East was Tom McClean of Ireland who rowed a 20 foot boat from Newfoundland to Ireland alone in 70 days 17 hours in 1969.

The longest jump ever made by a powerboat was achieved by Jerry Comeaux, 29, for a sequence in a James Bond movie, "Live and Let Die." He took off at a speed of 56 m.p.h. using a 135-h.p. Evinrude Starflite engine, and flew off of a greased ramp 110 feet through the air before landing.

The longest any man has ever jumped on water skis is 180 feet. Wayne Grimditch, 20, did this at Callaway Gardens, Pine Mountain, Georgia, in July, 1975. The first jump on water skis had been made by Ralph W. Samuelson off a greased ramp at Miami Beach, Florida, in 1928.

The longest ski jump ever recorded is one of 169 meters ($554\frac{1}{2}$ feet) by Heinz Wosipiwo of East Germany on a hill in Obersdorf, East Germany, on March 9, 1973.

Sonja Henie of Norway won the Olympic figure skating championship in 1928, 1932 and 1936, and went on to amass the greatest fortune in sports history. She starred in her own ice shows and eleven movies and earned an estimated $47,500,000.

Nino Bibbia of Italy has won virtually every title available in world-class toboggan racing. After capturing the gold medal in the 1948 Olympics, he went on to win 8 Grand National titles and 8 Curzon Cup titles, winning both titles in the years 1960-62-63-64. Tobogganers sometimes hurtle down the Cresta Run at St. Moritz, Switzerland, at speeds of 85 m.p.h.

An eight-man crew from the Adelaide High School Rowing Club rowed $101\frac{3}{4}$ miles on the Murray River in South Australia in 15 hours 1 minute on August 29, 1973, to set a marathon rowing mark.

Jack Beresford, Jr. of Great Britain is one of only four men who have taken home three gold medals in Olympic rowing competition. In addition, Beresford holds a record for his seven victories in the Wingfield Sculls competitions.

The world's tallest pagoda is the 326-foot-tall Shwe Dogon Pagoda in Rangoon, Burma, which was increased to its present height by the King of Ava in the late 18th century.

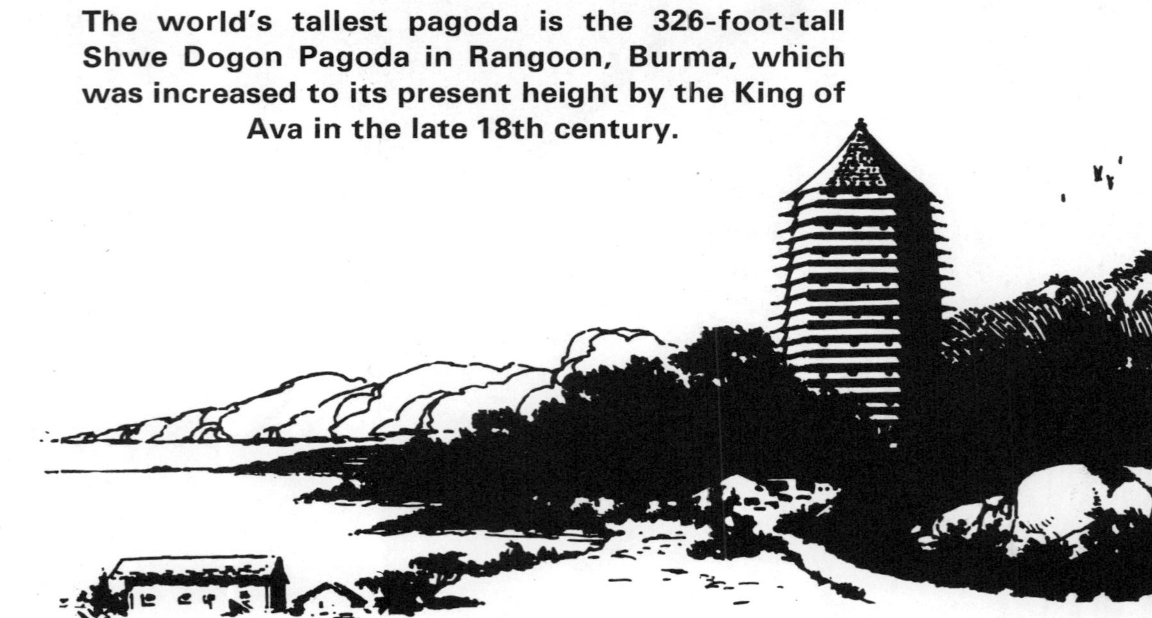

The oldest stained glass window in the world was made around the year 1050 A.D. It represents the Prophets of the Old Testament and is found in the cathedral of Augsburg in Bavaria, Germany.

The steepest wall in the world is the northwest stone face of Half Dome, in Yosemite National Park in California. It is 2,200 feet tall, 3,200 feet wide and the cliff is never more than 7 degrees away from a perfect vertical.

Mt. Everest, at 29,028 feet, has in this century proved the greatest challenge for mountain climbers. Since it was first conquered in 1953 by Edmund Hillary and Tenzing Norkhay, there have been 16 successful assaults. One of the most recent conquests was also the first time that any woman had stood atop Mt. Everest, the highest point on earth. Mrs. Junko Tabei, 34, of Japan, reached the summit on May 16, 1975.

The largest crater formed by a meteor crashing into the earth, Barringer Crater, was discovered in 1891 near Winslow, in northern Arizona. It is 4,150 feet across, and now is about 575 feet deep. Its parapet or edge rises 130 to 155 feet above the surrounding plain. It is believed that an iron-nickel mass from the skies with a diameter of 200 to 260 feet, weighing about 2,250,000 tons, gouged out the crater. The impact would have been equivalent to an explosion of 30 million tons of T.N.T.

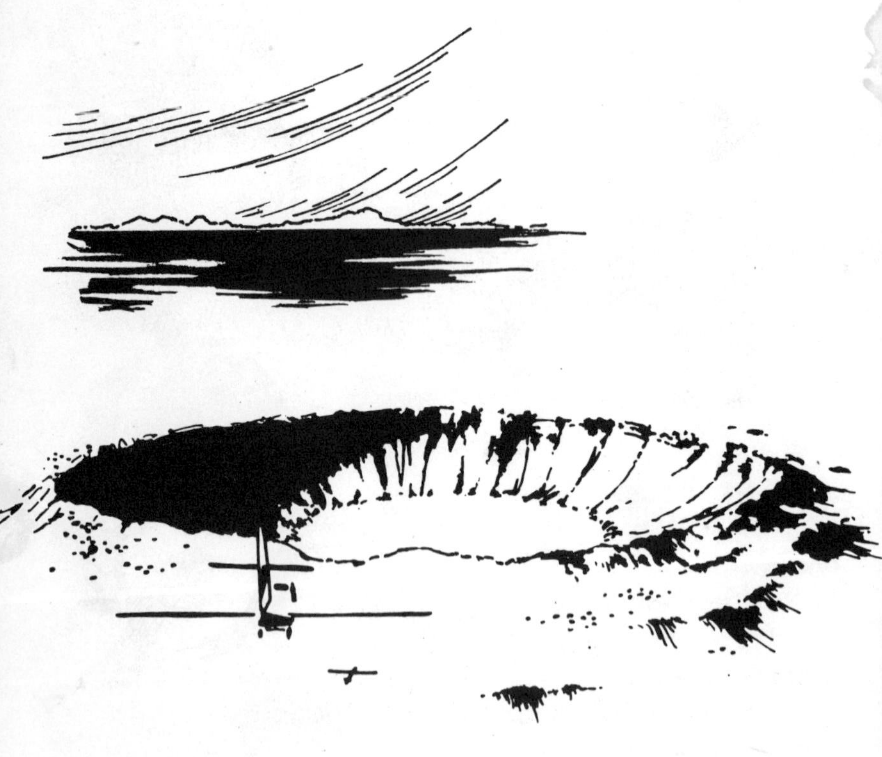

The largest meteorite ever found was one discovered in 1920 at Hoba West, near Grootfontein, in South-West Africa. It measured 9 feet in length and 8 feet in width and weighed 132,000 lbs. The largest ever exhibited in any museum is the 68,085-lb. meteorite discovered by Commander Robert Peary during his expedition to the North Pole and now shown in the Hayden Planetarium in New York City. It was known to the Eskimos as the Abnighito.

Although it is extremely difficult to measure the speed of fish accurately, the swordfish has become known for its very high speeds. One swordfish struck its bill through 22 inches of a ship's wooden side, and this indicated that the fish was swimming at a speed of 50 knots or 57.6 m.p.h.

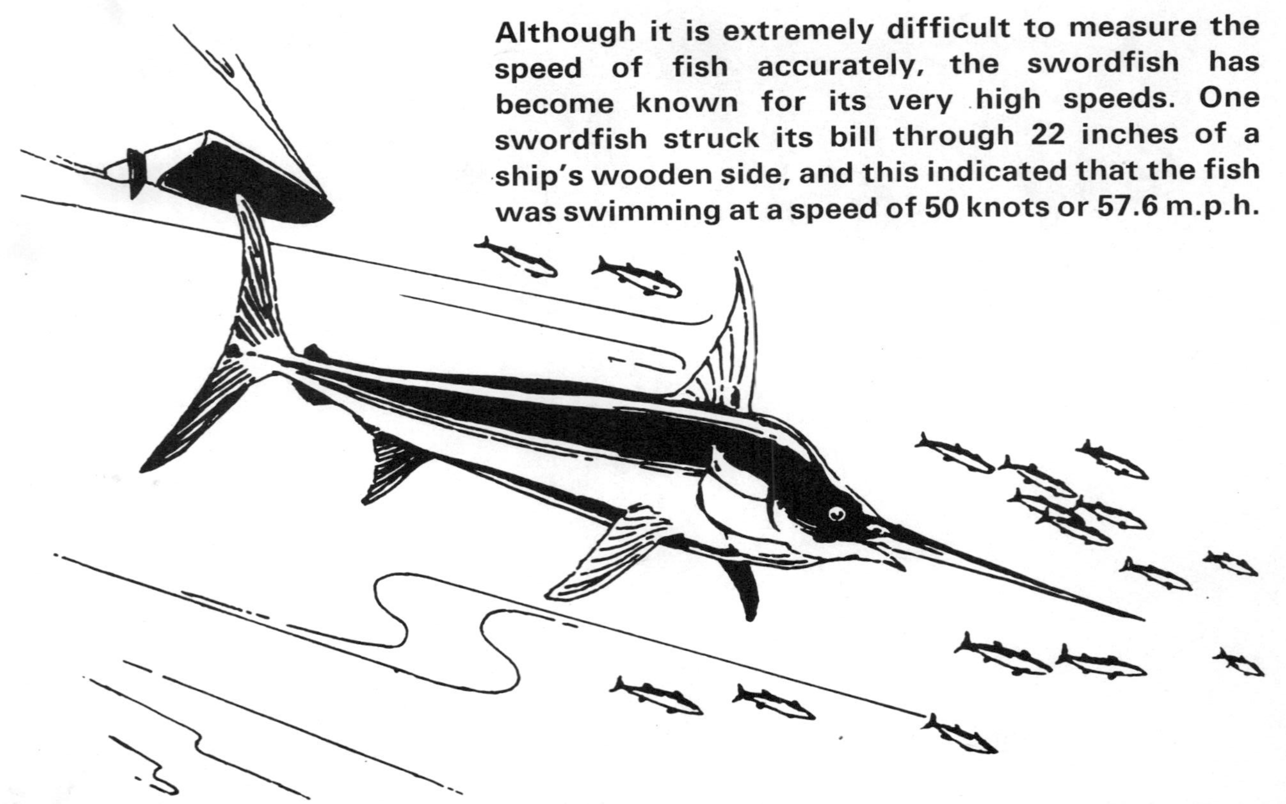

A sole-like fish was sighted from a diving submarine or bathyscaphe, called "Trieste," at a depth of 35,802 feet in the Challenger Deep, a trench in the western Pacific Ocean. This is more than 8,000 feet deeper than any fish had been seen or caught before. It happened on January 24, 1960, and the men inside were Dr. Jacques Piccard and Lt. Don Walsh of the U.S. Navy.

The largest single banquet course in the world is roasted camel, which is prepared occasionally for Bedouin wedding feasts. Cooked eggs are stuffed in fish, the fish stuffed in cooked chickens, the chickens stuffed into a roasted sheep carcass, and the sheep stuffed into a whole camel.

The World Record for eating hard-boiled eggs belongs to Stanley Judge of Hull, Humberside, England, who consumed 12 in 103 seconds on September 23, 1974.

The doughnut-eating champion of the world is Mike Musselman of Roy, Utah, who devoured 27 doughnuts in 7 minutes 16 seconds on February 5, 1975.

The U.S.S.R. claims the most doctors within its borders with 555,400 in 1969, or one for every 433 persons. But one country has a higher proportion of physicians – Israel, one doctor for every 400 inhabitants in 1970, for a total of 7,281.

The Goodyear Airship hangar in Akron, Ohio, is 1,175 feet long, 325 feet wide and 200 feet high. The largest hangar in the world, it covers 8.35 acres of ground and has an interior capacity of 55,000,000 cubic feet.

The Modern Pentathlon (riding, fencing, shooting, swimming, and running) was first introduced into the program of the Olympic Games in 1912. The greatest performer in Olympic history is Andras Balczo of Hungary with gold medals in 1960, 1968, and 1972. Balczo also has won a record six world titles.

If you are a good surfer, you can ride a wave as far as it can take you. Nearly 5,700 feet is the longest. About 4 to 6 times a year rideable surfing waves break at Matanchen Bay near San Blas, Nayarit, Mexico, which challenge the best surfers to ride that long.

James Gowan set a world record when he became a judge in Canada at the age of 27 years 26 days. Born in Ireland in 1815, he was Sir James Gowan, K.C.M.G. when he died at the age of 94.

David Kwan, 22, set off on foot from Singapore on May 4, 1957, and finally arrived in London, England, 81 weeks later, to set the mark for the longest hike ever recorded. He traveled 18,500 miles through 14 countries and averaged 32 miles a day.

Bill Robinson, the American actor and tap dancer, recorded the fastest time ever for running 100 yards backwards. It took him only 13.5 seconds.

The longest fence in the world stretches 3,437 miles—long enough to connect Seattle, Washington, with Miami, Florida. It encloses the main sheep grazing areas of Queensland, Australia. The 6-foot-high wire fence protects the sheep from Australia's wild dogs or dingoes.

Raising sheep in Australia is a big business, and it is no surprise to learn that the largest sheep ranch (or sheep station as it is called in Australia and New Zealand) is an area of 4,080 square miles in the northwest part of South Australia. It supports between 70,000 and 90,000 head of sheep, 700 cattle, and an additional 25,000 uninvited kangaroos.

A mother with 69 children? Yes, it happened in the mid-1800's when the first wife of a Russian peasant, Fyodor Vassilet, gave birth to 16 pairs of twins, 7 sets of triplets and 4 sets of quadruplets. Mme. Vassilet became so famous that she was presented at the court of the Russian Czar, Alexander II.

The largest single litter a cat ever had was 13 kittens, but one cat named "Dusty," who lived in Bonham, Texas, set an all-time record by giving birth to 420 kittens in her 17 years.

The hot-dog eating champion is Raymond Kowalski, 21, who ate twenty 2-oz. frankfurters in 4 minutes 47 seconds on February 28, 1974.

A sausage 3,124 feet long was made by 30 English butchers on June 29, 1966. They used 728 lbs. of pork and 167 lbs. of cereal and seasoning.

Billiards has been played as a game since 1429 in France, but it was not until about 1850 that it was widely played. The earliest championship match was held in 1870 at St. James's Hall in London, England. The hall was filled to capacity that night.

Only once in the 67-year history of the American Bowling Congress has a perfect game of 300 been achieved in the Classic team event. It was rolled by Les Schissler of Denver in the 1967 tournament.

The retail prices of the world's most expensive perfumes tend to be set for publicity reasons and are not a reliable indicator of how rare or popular any one perfume actually is. However, the most expensive ingredient used in making perfume is pure French middle note Jasmine essence, which sells for $6,960 per kilogram or $197 per ounce.

Do you believe that anyone can blow 169 smoke rings from a single inhalation of a cigarette? Keith Harraway of Essex, England, set this record on July 12, 1974.

Diamonds are the hardest known naturally occurring minerals, and one of the most valuable. The Hope diamond, now on display in the Smithsonian Institution, Washington, D.C., weighs 44.4 carats and is the largest known blue diamond. Blue and pink are the rarest colors for diamonds.

For 30 seconds, Scott Case puffed simultaneously on 110 cigarettes at the Oddball Olympics held in Los Angeles in April, 1974.

The biggest man ever to step inside a professional boxing ring was Gogea Mitu of Rumania, who in 1935 stood 7 feet 4 inches tall and weighed in at 327 lbs. Jim Cully of Ireland (shown here) also stood 7 feet 4 inches tall, but weighed only 273 lbs. He lost all of his four professional bouts in 1947-48.

The longest marathon for tennis singles ever played by two players is 30 hours 30 minutes by Sandy Goss and Rita Santarpia of Beltsville, Maryland, May 10-11, 1975. Linford Stillson of Danbury, Connecticut, played singles against a number of different opponents for 80 hours, May 16-20, 1975.

The penknife with the greatest number of blades is the Year Knife. It was constructed in the year 1822 with 1,822 blades. Each year a blade is added so it had 1,975 in 1975. It will continue to be made to match the number of blades to the year until 2000 A.D., when it will be completely filled.

The longest time canned food stayed in the can was about 135 years. It happened this way. In 1823, some beef was canned in England, and put aboard the British ship "Fury," which was sunk in the Northwest Passage, Canada. On December 11, 1958, the can finally was opened after the ship was salvaged.

Tim Knappen stood on his hands for 45 minutes 42.3 seconds during the Oddball Olympics held in Los Angeles in 1974. It was a world record for handstanding.

William Charlton walked 15 miles 1,738 yards at Davenport, Tasmania, on June 4, 1972, all the while balancing an empty pint milk bottle on the top of his head.

Nylon stockings are supposed to be sheer, and the sheerest normally available are 9 denier. In 1956, stockings were exhibited in London that were made from 6-denier yarn, the sheerest nylons ever made. Compare this with a strand of hair from the average human head, which is about 50 denier.

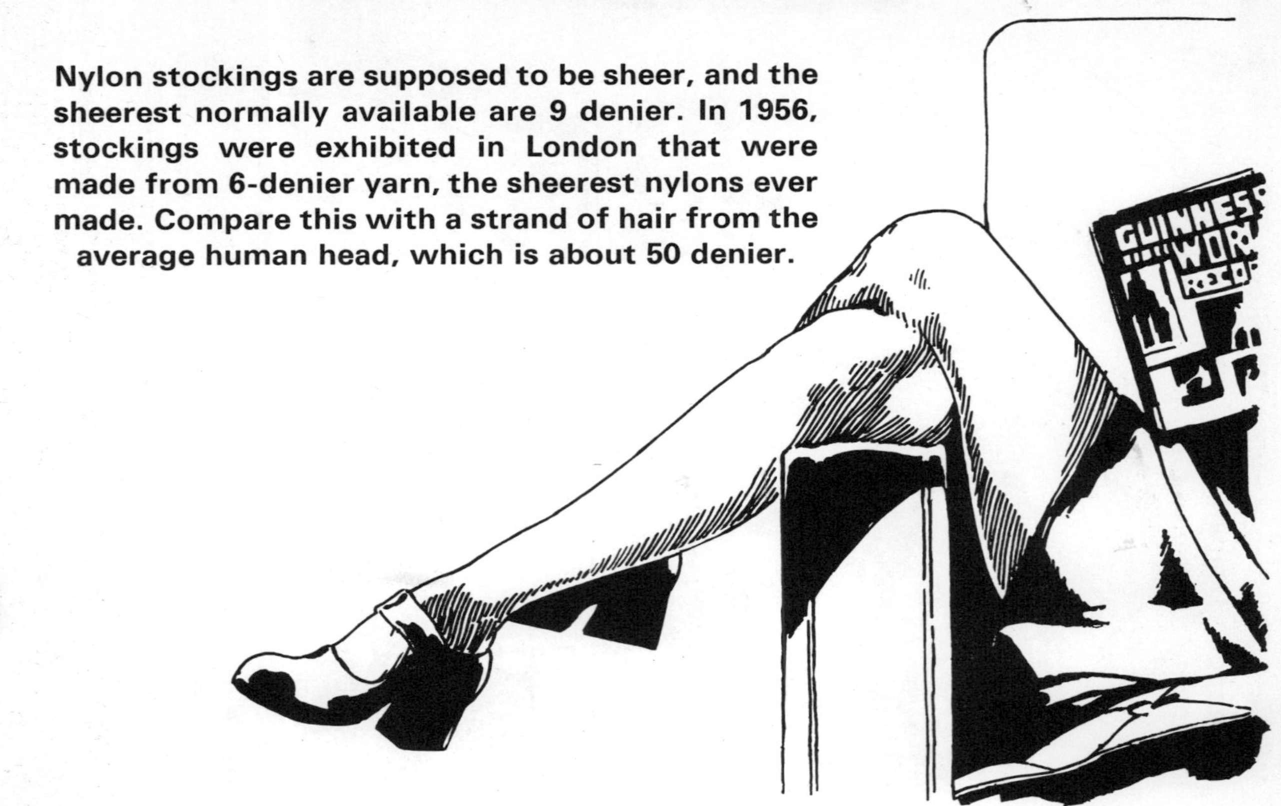

Try not to get into an argument with Alfred West (born in London, England, in 1901). West has successfully split a single human hair 13 times into 14 separate strands. That's splitting hairs!

When Dean Martin signed a three-year no-option contract with N.B.C. for a reported $34,000,000, it was the largest television contract on record. In 1968, Martin was acclaimed as the top earning show business personality of all time with $5,000,000 in one year.

The movie with the highest gross earnings in the world is "The Godfather," which earned $155 million between March, 1972, and February, 1974. Marlon Brando was paid $10 million to play the title role—the greatest amount ever earned by an actor for a single film. "Jaws," which grossed $14,000,000 in its first week, compared to $10,000,000 in "The Godfather's" first week, may go on to set a new record for gross earnings.

Ralph Charell, a network television executive in New York, claims that he has successfully collected for every misadventure that has ever damaged him. His total receipts in settlement for such complaints as poor telephone and car rental service, gas and electric overcharges, failure to deliver on time, imperfect goods, improper installation, and the like have amounted to $76,919.31 as of July 1, 1975—and he is still complaining when it is justified.

The Swiss started yodeling in the Alps, but the champion who has given out with the longest yodel is an Englishman named Bill Gore. For 5 hours 3 minutes on January 9, 1975, the whole city of Birmingham, England, heard his song.

A toy balloon set a flight record by traveling 9,000 miles. It took less than 20 days after it was released by Jane Dorst from Atherton, California, on May 21, 1972, to reach Pietermaritzburg, South Africa on June 10, 1972.

The most kites ever flown on a single string is 261 by William R. Bigge at Burtonville, Maryland, on October 5, 1974.

The World Championship of bridge, the Bermuda Bowl, has been won most often by Italy's "Blue Team" with 13 triumphs. The same team has also won 3 Olympic championships. Giorgio Belladonna (shown here) was on all 16 of these winning teams.

Pi is the number of times the diameter of a circle goes into its circumference. It never works out evenly (it is 22 divided by 7) and it can be carried out to thousands of decimal places. Michael John Poultney, a student in Cleveland, England, memorized the first 3,025 places and recited them aloud in front of 200 witnesses, including a reporter and a recorder, in October, 1974.

Covered bridges haven't been built since cars were invented, but the longest in the world is at Hartland, New Brunswick, Canada. It was completed in 1899 and measures 1,282 feet in length.

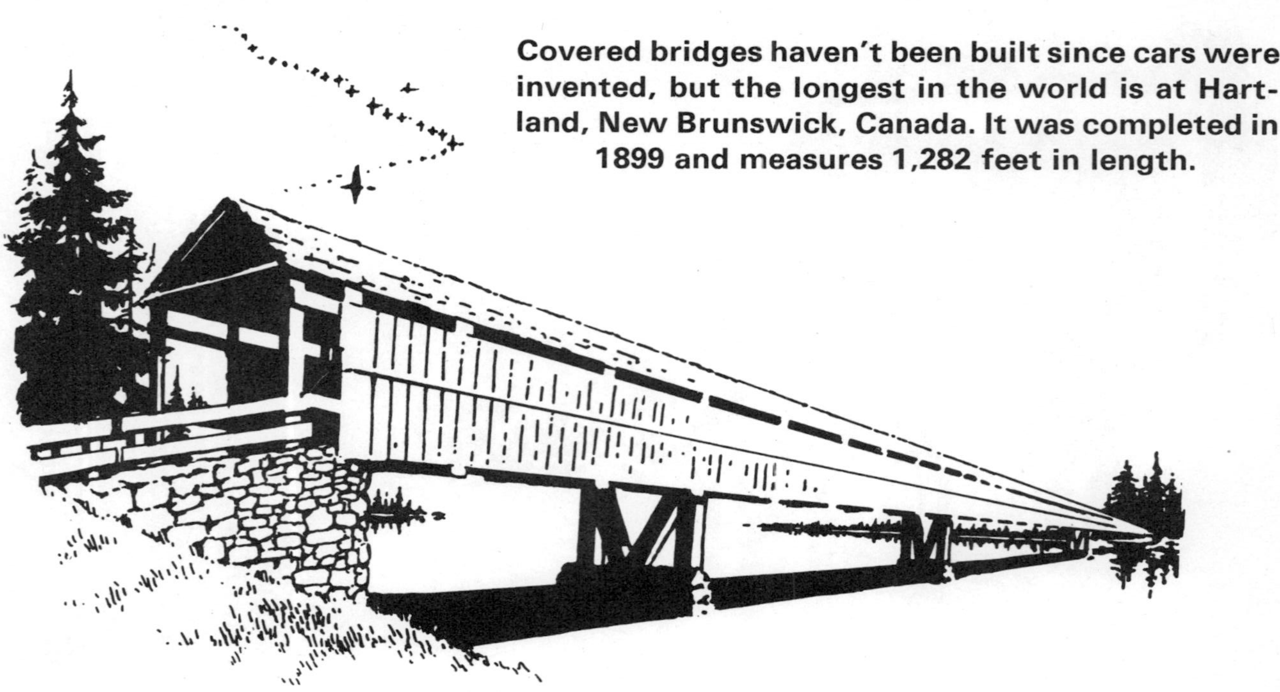

The highest suspension bridge in the world spans the gap over the Royal Gorge of the Arkansas River in Colorado. It stands 1,053 feet above the water level and has a main span of 880 feet. It took only 6 months to build, construction ending on December 6, 1929.

Every spring colleges around the country graduate their senior classes. One part of the ceremony usually honors a celebrated man or woman with a degree in recognition of outstanding achievement or service to the particular school or to the country as a whole. The greatest number of honorary degrees awarded to any individual is 89, given to Herbert Hoover, the President of the United States from 1929 to 1933, the years of the Great Depression.

Scottish-born Andrew Carnegie came to the United States to make his fortune. He began his career working in a factory for $1.20 a week. Eventually, he did so well that he owned steel mills and in the last 18 years of his life (1901-19), he gave away more in gifts than anyone before him—about $350,000,000, when the dollar was worth much more than it is today. The gifts included 7,689 church organs and 2,811 libraries.

The highest dive regularly made is from rocks 118 feet high by professional divers in Acapulco, Mexico. The rocks, which are at the base of La Quebrada ("the break in the rocks"), jut out 21 feet, so the divers must also leap 27 feet forward from the take-off point. They land in water that is only 12 feet deep.

The world's largest bonfire was built at College Station, Texas, on Thanksgiving Eve, 1969, and rose to a height of 107 feet 10 inches.

The worst marine disaster involving a single ship occurred when the 25,484-ton "Wilhelm Gustloff" was torpedoed by a Russian submarine on January 30, 1945. It resulted in a loss of about 7,700 lives.

The world's greatest lifeguard was a deaf-mute named Leroy Colombo, who saved 907 people from drowning in the waters around Galveston Island, Texas, from 1917 to his own death in 1974. The people of Galveston commemorated his accomplishments with a plaque which was unveiled in November, 1974.

This monster ice cream sundae of more than 3,956 lbs. was built with a large crowd watching at Farrell's Ice Cream Parlour Restaurant in McLean, Virginia, on July 13, 1975. It contained 777 gallons of ice cream and was smothered with 6 gallons of chocolate sauce, $1\frac{1}{4}$ gallons of whipped cream, one case of chocolate sprinkles, and a dish of cherry halves, representing a grand total of 2,099,895 calories.

The largest Easter egg ever was made in Australia in April, 1974. It was 6 feet high, 13 feet $3\frac{1}{2}$ inches in circumference and weighed 648 lbs.

The longest pair of elephant tusks ever recorded (excluding prehistoric examples) are a pair from the eastern Congo (Zaire) now kept in the Bronx Zoo in New York City. One measures 11 feet $5\frac{1}{2}$ inches along the outside curve and the other measures 11 feet. Together they weigh 293 lbs.

Long hair isn't a new thing. The longest hair on record belonged to Swami Pandarasannadhi of India. In 1949 it was said to be 26 feet long, matted and tangled, and a home for all kinds of bugs and lice.

Livestock prices hit an all-time low in South Africa in 1934, where you could buy a donkey for less than 4 pence (4 cents).

Evelyn Patterson of Zambia holds the women's deep-diving record. In 1967 she descended to 125 feet below the surface while holding her breath.

The shortest scheduled airplane flight made since 1967 is one by Loganair between the Orkney Islands (Scotland) of Westray and Papa Westray. Though scheduled for 2 minutes, with a favorable wind it can be accomplished in only 69 seconds.

The tallest kind of cactus in the world is the saguaro, which is found in Arizona, New Mexico, California, and Sonora, Mexico. One cactus found near Madrona, New Mexico, in 1950 measured 53 feet from the base to the tip of its tallest branch. The saguaro has waxy white blooms which are followed by edible crimson fruit.

The duration record for go-go dancing is 110 hours (with 5-minute breaks each hour), made by Patricia Glenister in Leicester, England, in May, 1975.

The highest tribute at a performance of a ballet or an opera is when the audience applauds and calls the performers back on stage after the curtain has come down. In October, 1964, after a performance of the Ballet "Swan Lake" at the National Opera House in Vienna, Austria, the principal dancers, Margot Fonteyn and Rudolf Nureyev, were applauded for a total of 89 curtain calls, the most ever received by any performer.

The largest book in the world is bigger than your bed. Containing a verse story called "The Little Red Elf" written by William P. Wood, who also designed, constructed and printed the book, it stands 7 feet 2 inches high and measures 10 feet across when open. At present, it is on display in a case near Dunoon, Scotland.

The narrowest street in the world is St. John's Lane in Rome, which is only 19 inches wide. The smallest "park" in the world once was Mills End Park, on a safety island in the middle of Front Street, Portland, Oregon. It was set aside as a colony for leprechauns, and as a site for snail races.

Jiving non-stop for 42 hours 30 minutes (with 5-minute breaks per hour for massage and rest) is the record set by Ken Troy and partners in Winnipeg, Canada, in May, 1975.

The largest playable guitar stands 8 feet 10 inches tall, weighs 80 lbs. and has a volume of 16,000 cubic inches (as compared with 1,024 cubic inches in the standard size). It was built in 1970 by a company in Chicago and carries a hefty $15,000 price tag.

The only performer in history able to juggle, as opposed to "shower," 10 balls or 8 plates was the Italian Enrico Rastelli, who lived from 1896 to 1931.

When a whip is "cracked," the end is made to travel above the speed of sound, which is 760 m.p.h. The longest stock whip ever "cracked" is one 80 feet long, first cracked by Frank Dean at the North Dakota State Fair in 1939.

INDEX

advertising sign, largest, 13
balloon, toy, longest flight, 68
banquet, largest dish, 34
billiards, earliest match, 50
bonfire, largest, 77
book, largest, 90
bottle balancing, longest distance, 61
bowling, perfect game, 51
boxer, tallest, 56
bridge (contract), most wins, 70
cactus, tallest, 87
candy, highest consumption, 6
canned food, oldest, 59
cat, most prolific, 47
complainer, most successful, 66
covered bridge, longest, 72
crater, largest meteor, 30
curtain calls, most, 89
deep-sea diver, woman, 85
diamond, rarest, 54
disaster, worst marine, 78
disease, most common, 7
dive, highest regularly performed, 76
doctors, most in country, 37
highest proportion, 37
dog, oldest, 9
dog sled race, fastest, 8
doughnuts, eating, 36
Easter egg, largest, 81
eggs, hard-boiled, eating, 35
escapist, 2
fence, longest, 44
fishes, deepest, 33
fishes, fastest, 32
flight, shortest scheduled airplane, 86
go-go dancing, marathon, 88
guitar, largest, 93
hair, longest, 83
hair splitting, most times, 63
hamburger, largest, 11
handstand, longest, 60
hangar, largest, 38
hike, longest, 42
honorary degrees, most, 74
Hope diamond, 54
hot dog, eating, 48
ice cream sundae, biggest, 80
ice skater, most successful, 22
jive dancing, marathon, 92
judge, youngest, 41
juggler, best, 94
kites flown, most simultaneously, 69
knife, most bladed, 58
lifeguard, greatest, 79
lighthouse, most remote, 14
livestock prices, lowest, 84
memorizing pi, 75
meteorite, largest discovered, 30
meteorite, largest exhibited, 31
mine, deepest, 16
monument, tallest, 12
mother, most prolific, 46
mountaineer, highest woman, 29
Mt. Everest, conquest of, 29
movie actor, highest paid, 65
nylons, sheerest, 62
pagoda, tallest, 26
Pentathlon, modern, 39
perfume, most expensive, 52
philanthropist, greatest, 75
pizza, largest, 10
powerboat jump, longest, 19
rowing, marathon, 24
rowing, most gold medals, 25
rowing, transatlantic, first, 18
running backwards, fastest, 43
sausage, longest, 49
sheep ranch (station), largest, 45
ski jump, longest, 21
smoke rings, most, 53
smoking cigarettes, most, 55
stained glass windows, oldest, 27
street, narrowest, 91
surfing wave, longest, 40
suspension bridge, longest, 73
tennis singles, marathon, 57
toboggan racing, most titles, 23
tree, loneliest, 15
tusks, largest, 82
TV personality, highest paid, 64
volcano, highest dormant, 17
wall, steepest, 28
water ski jump, longest, 20
whip, longest cracked, 95